STEPHANIE WILKINS

Kitchen Vibe

Flavorful Foods that
Make You Feel Good

Cover Photographs by Darque Room Images

ISBN 979-8-35093-257-7

Contents

Introduction

Picture this... music, singing (very loud), great food smells, lively conversation, and plenty of laughter. That's the vibe in my kitchen.

The kitchen is my happy place. Not just because I love to eat, but also because food is a way of showing love and bringing people together. My happiest moments are when I am preparing a meal to share with others.

I started on this cookbook journey to share the recipes that I grew up eating and the favorite dishes that are constantly requested by friends and family. Throughout this book, I share stories that inspired certain recipes and suggestions for creating good flavorful food for one person or a meal to share.

As a wife, mom, and full-time professional in the workforce, I recognize that life can be hectic and most days there is not much time to cook or prepare food. Oh, and let's not forget the people that don't like or even know how to cook. Well, help is on the way, because I have written some quick "go-to" recipes and dishes that are easy to prepare in a matter of minutes. Busy person, new to cooking, or seasoned home chef, regardless of where your time or cooking skills are, I have got you covered. You will find dishes with a variety of ingredients and cooking times but no need to spend all day in the kitchen, I promise.

I am so thrilled to share this cookbook with you and my desire is for you to find your kitchen vibe with some new recipes that motivate you to cook for yourself or with your loved ones more frequently. So, crack open this book and check out some recipes, get your kitchen essentials out, put some music on, and let's start cooking.

Much Love

Stephanie

You Gotta Have These!

Kitchen Essentials

Whether you are new to cooking or already know your way around the kitchen, good kitchen tools are essential. No need to have fancy gadgets. Just having some sustainable basic tools will make your cooking experience more enjoyable. So, before you dive into the recipes, we've got some work to do. First, take inventory of the cooking items you already have. Second, check out my list of kitchen essentials. Lastly, get your kitchen set up with all of essential cooking tools. Now, we are ready to start cooking.

Knife set: Regardless of how much you cook, knives are probably one of the most essential tools that you can have, so it might be worth it to invest in a good set.

Measuring Cups and Spoons: Every kitchen needs measuring cups and spoons.

Cast Iron Skillet: Love, love, love this skillet because you can use it to cook and bake just about anything and it also transfers from the stove top to the oven.

Dutch Oven: Another versatile pot that transfers from the stove top to the oven. Very good for searing meats, cooking chicken, soups/chili, pasta, and even bread.

Nonstick Frying Pan: Pancakes, eggs, or fish, this will be your go-to item for cooking anything that may stick to the pan.

Cutting Board: For slicing, dicing, or chopping, you need to have a nice cutting board in your kitchen.

Instant-read thermometer: Grilling, stove top, oven, or air fryer, this tool will take the guesswork out of when your meats and poultry are done.

Baking sheets: This will be your go-to pan for basic oven needs.

Set of Bowls: These are a multi-purpose item for mixing or storing food that you can't do without.

Blender and/or Food Processor: You got to have this item for whipping up smoothies, soups, and just about everything in between.

Disinfect Wipes or Spray: No cross-contamination in your kitchen. It's an essential item to keep your countertop and kitchen surroundings clean and sanitized.

The "B" Word
Breakfast

Let's talk about the "B" word. It's ok, you can say it. Breakfast! What kind of B person are you? Are you a "B" first thing in the morning, or a "B" for dinner? Regardless of where you fall in the "B" person category, I have some delicious and easy breakfast options for you. Try my Omg! French toast or oatmeal pancakes for a tasty big breakfast, or a jazzed-up smoothie if you need something fast. Weekend brunch is a breeze with some egg stuff and pumpkin patch muffins. Then sometimes, you just feel like being a "B" all day long, so whip up some crunchy homemade granola or peanut buttery banana bread to snack on. Go ahead and be a "B" person with these recipes. I guarantee everyone will love you.

Mouth Watering Buttermilk Waffles

Delicious Oatmeal Pancakes

Egg Stuff

OMG! French Toast

Jazzed Up Smoothies

Pumpkin Patch Muffins

Peanut Buttery Banana Bread

Crunchy Homemade Granola

Mouth Watering Butter Milk Waffles

5

Mouth Watering Butter Milk Waffles

Everything you crave in a waffle. Crisp on the outside, light and fluffy inside with a delicious hint of butter and vanilla throughout.

2 eggs

1 ¾ c. buttermilk

½ c. butter, melted

2 tsp. vanilla extract

¼ c. granulated sugar

2 tsp. baking powder

1 tsp. baking soda

¼ tsp salt

2 c. all-purpose flour

Whisk eggs, buttermilk, and sugar together until smooth. Whisk in vanilla extract and melted butter. Sift together flour, baking powder, and baking soda and add it to the wet ingredients. Add salt and stir all ingredients together until evenly combined. Let batter sit for 10-15 minutes while preheating the waffle maker. Lightly grease the waffle maker with cooking spray and cook waffles according to your waffle maker instructions.

Jazz It Up: Add ½ c. fresh or frozen blueberries to the batter for some delicious blueberry waffles. Or, top waffles with breaded or battered fried chicken pieces and drizzle with warm syrup.

Delicious Oatmeal Pancakes

Breakfast just got better because oatmeal goodness is combined with hot fluffy pancakes. Whip up this recipe, pile them high, slather on some butter, add some fruit if you like and let the syrup drip down the sides. A delicious way to start your day.

1 c. old fashion oats

1 ¼ c. buttermilk*

2 T. granu-
lated sugar

1 egg

¾ tsp. vanilla extract

⅔ c. all-purpose flour

2 tsp. baking powder

¼ tsp. salt

2 T. butter, melted. Butter for serving and greasing the pan

In a large bowl, combine oats and buttermilk. Allow the mixture to sit at room temperature for 15 minutes for the oats to soften. Add sugar, egg, melted butter, and vanilla to the oat mixture. Whisk until thoroughly combined. Add flour, baking powder, salt and mix well until combined. Be careful not to over-mix. Set aside while you preheat a nonstick pan. Place the nonstick pan over medium-low heat and grease with butter. Using a ⅓ c. measuring cup, pour the batter onto the pan, slightly spreading it. Cook until light golden brown, then flip and continue cooking until cooked through.

Cooking Tip: *You can use regular milk as a buttermilk substitute. You may need to increase the flour by 2-3 T. if the batter is too thin.

Egg Stuff

You might be wondering... what in the world is egg stuff? I was feeling creative one morning and decided to prepare a breakfast casserole for a family brunch. Well, my brother, (Michael) named the breakfast casserole egg stuff because I guess he didn't know what to call it, he just kept saying "this egg stuff is really good." And guess what? Everyone in the family started calling it egg stuff. After that brunch years ago egg stuff has truly become a family favorite. It is also an easy meal that comes together in no time with eggs, sausage, cheese, and anything else that you want to put in it. So, whenever company comes to my house you can count on some egg stuff for breakfast or brunch.

3 slices bread w/o crust (optional)
Butter
1 lb. bulk sausage
2 c. grated cheese
6 eggs
1 pt. half and half cream
1 tsp. salt
1 tsp. dry mustard

Lightly butter bread on both sides. Place bread in the bottom of a 9x13-inch pan. Over medium heat, brown and drain sausage. Put it on top of the bread. Sprinkle with grated cheese. Combine eggs, half and half cream, dry mustard, and salt. Beat well. Pour into pan over bread and sausage. Bake at 350 degrees for 30 minutes.

Jazz It Up: Eliminate the bread and use 4 cups of prepared shredded hash browns on the bottom of the pan. Or change the add-ins according to what you like. Any chopped meat, cheese or veggie will work.

Omg! French Toast

You don't have to be skilled in the kitchen to make this breakfast item. This quick and easy recipe will turn out delicious every single time. My secret ingredient is the sprinkle of cinnamon sugar. Serve with your favorite topping or eat it plain. Omg!

6 slices of bread
2 eggs
½ c. half and half

1 tsp. vanilla extract
2 T. brown sugar, packed
¼ tsp. cinnamon

cooking oil of choice
2 T. butter or spread
cinnamon sugar

In a large bowl, whisk together eggs, half/half, vanilla, brown sugar, and cinnamon until smooth. Set aside. Preheat a large cooking pan over medium to low heat. Add a small amount of cooking oil and spread it evenly in the pan. Working with one slice at a time, dip each slice of bread into the egg mixture and flip until it is nicely soaked. Then place battered bread into the oiled pan and cook for about 2-3 minutes or until each side is lightly brown and the center is firm. Repeat the batter and cooking process with the remaining bread. Lightly butter each piece of cooked French toast, then sprinkle with cinnamon sugar.

Jazzed Up Smoothie

Easy, Easy, Easy! The best part about home-made smoothies is that you can have fun and tailor it to your taste and diet. They are full of health benefits and a good way to get a lot of nutrients. Go ahead and give it a try. I guarantee you are going to love this smoothie!

2 c. frozen fruit (I like strawberries and bananas)
1 c. water
¼ c. yogurt
1 packet of sweetener
2 T. sugar-free vanilla pudding

In a blender, combine fruit, liquid, yogurt, sweetener, and sugar-free pudding. Add small amounts of liquid while blending until it looks creamy and the desired consistency is reached. Pour into your favorite glass, add a straw, and enjoy.

Add in whatever you like: fresh fruit, fruit juice, almond milk, nuts or nut butter, protein powder or drink, kale, or spinach.

Pumpkin Patch Muffins

Sugar and spice and everything yummy. This recipe has just the right amount of pumpkin flavor, guaranteed to become your new favorite breakfast or snack.

1 ½ c. all-purpose flour
1 tsp. baking soda
¾ tsp. ground ginger
½ tsp. baking powder
½ tsp. cinnamon

¼ tsp. salt
⅛ tsp. ground cloves
1 c. sugar
3 oz. box sugar-free vanilla pudding
1 c. canned pumpkin

¼ c. packed brown sugar
2 T. canola oil
1 egg
cooking spray muffin pan and liners

Preheat oven to 375 F. Combine flour and next 6 ingredients (through cloves), stir well with a whisk. In a large bowl, combine granulated sugar and the next 5 ingredients (through eggs), beat with a mixer at medium speed until well blended about 2 minutes. Add flour mixture to sugar mixture, and beat until combined. Place 12 muffin liners in a muffin pan, and coat liners with cooking spray. Divide batter evenly among prepared cups. Bake at 375 degrees for 25 minutes or until muffins spring back when touched lightly in the center. Remove the muffin pan and place it on a cooling rack.

Peanut Buttery Banana Bread

It doesn't get any better than peanut butter and bananas. Easy, moist, and delicious with a hint of nutty goodness. This recipe is perfect for using up those over ripe bananas and will make you hungry while it is in the oven. Serve it up for brunch or as a snack.

1 ½ c. mashed ripe bananas

⅓ c. sour cream.

3 T. butter, melted

2 eggs

½ tsp. vanilla extract

½ c. granulated sugar

½ c. brown sugar

1½ c. all-purpose flour

¾ tsp. baking soda

½ tsp. salt

½ tsp. cinnamon

⅛ tsp. allspice

Preheat oven to 350 F. To prepare bread, combine the first 5 ingredients in a large bowl, and beat with a mixer at medium speed. Add granulated and brown sugars, and beat until blended. Combine flour and next 4 ingredients (to allspice) in a small bowl. Add flour mixture to banana mixture, and beat until blended. Pour batter into a 9x5-inch loaf pan coated with cooking spray. Bake for 1 hour or until a wooded toothpick inserted in the center comes out clean. Remove the bread from the oven, and cool for 10 minutes in the pan. Remove from the pan to cool.

CREAMY PEANUT BUTTER GLAZE

⅓ c. powdered sugar

1 T. low-fat milk

1 T. creamy peanut butter

Combine powdered sugar, milk, and 1 T. peanut butter in a small bowl. Whisk until creamy. Drizzle over bread.

Crunchy Homemade Granola

Great for breakfast or a quick healthy snack. This homemade granola will become your new favorite for anytime of the day.

2 c. old fashion oats	***½ c. chopped pecans**	**¼ c. butter, melted**
1 c. shredded sweetened	**2 T. brown sugar**	**½ c. maple syrup**
Coconut	**1 tsp. cinnamon**	**1 ½ tsp. vanilla extract**
*½ c. chopped walnuts	**½ tsp. sea salt**	***⅓ c. dried cranberries**

Preheat oven to 300 F. Line a large baking pan with parchment paper. Set aside. In a large bowl, combine oats, coconut, walnuts, pecans, brown sugar, cinnamon, and sea salt. In a small saucepan, melt the butter over medium heat, stirring occasionally until butter turns golden brown. Remove from heat and add the maple syrup mixture over dry ingredients. Stir until well combined. Pour the granola mixture onto the prepared baking sheet. Spread granola into an even layer. Bake for 35 minutes or until granola is golden brown, stirring every 10 minutes. Remove from oven and stir in dried cranberries. Let the granola cool completely. Store in a zip-lock bag or airtight container for up to 1 month.

Note: *Any type of dried fruit or nuts can be used in this recipe.

Snack Attack

Appetizers and Snacks

Truth be told... I am a snacker! It doesn't matter what the event is or the time of day, give me some snacks and I will be happy. Variety is the key, so I pulled together some of my favorites that are distinctly different and always delicious. So, grab that little appetizer plate and load it up with these fun foods. It's snack time.

Royal Green Goddess Dip

Teriyaki Meatballs

Lemon Pepper Wings

Easy Caprese

Cheesy Crab Dip

Chicken Zucchini Minis

Royal Green Goddess Dip

Smooth, creamy, and full of fresh herbs. This versatile dip is perfect for entertaining and can also be used as a salad dressing. It also tastes great on top of steak or chicken.

2 T. fresh dill	1 tsp. dried tarragon	2 scallions, chopped	½ tsp. ground pepper
½ c. fresh mint	1 clove garlic	¼ c. sour cream	¼ tsp. kosher salt
1 c. fresh parsley	½ c. mayonnaise	1 T. lemon juice	
½ c. fresh spinach	½ c. ricotta cheese	1 tsp. honey	

Place all ingredients in a food processor or blender, and pulse 8 to 10 times until well combined. Scrape the mixture into a bowl or serving dish. Cover and chill for 30 minutes. Serve with veggies, crackers or chips. It is just that easy!

Teriyaki Meatballs

You can't have appetizers without meatballs and homemade meatballs are extra special. I know what you are thinking... making meatballs from scratch will take too much time. Give me 30 minutes and I promise you will have homemade meatballs smothered in a fantastic teriyaki sauce that will have you licking your fingers.

Meatballs	1 tsp. ground ginger	½ c. plain	½ c. soy sauce
1-2 lbs. ground beef (80% meat, 20% fat)	1 scallion finely chopped	panko breadcrumbs	2 T. maple syrup
	2 eggs	⅓ c. milk	1 T. apple cider vinegar
⅓ c. grated parmesan cheese	2 T. soy sauce		¼ c. hoisin sauce
	1 T. brown sugar	**Sauce**	½ tsp. ginger
1 tsp. garlic powder		⅓ c. brown sugar	1 ½ tsp cornstarch

Preheat oven to 400 F. Add all meatball ingredients to a large bowl and use your hands to mix together. Then form the mixture into approximately 18 meatballs. Line a baking sheet with aluminum foil and set the meatballs ½ inch apart on the sheet. Bake for 20 minutes.

While the meatballs are baking, make the sauce. In a skillet pan, whisk brown sugar, soy sauce, syrup, vinegar, hoisin sauce, ginger, and cornstarch together on medium heat. The sauce will thicken quickly in about 15 seconds. Remove from heat, add meatballs to the sauce, and stir so that they are coated. Jazz it up with scallions as a garnish (optional) serve warm and enjoy!

Teriyaki
Meatballs

17

Lemon Pepper Wings

Lemon pepper wings are my absolute favorite way to eat chicken wings and after you try my easy recipe, I bet they will become your favorite too. No mega cooking skills or frying needed to make these wings. Only five ingredients, bake them in the oven and you will have the perfect appetizer or weekday meal.

2 lbs. chicken wing parts
2 T. olive oil
¼ c. lemon pepper seasoning
2 T. corn starch
1 tsp salt

Preheat oven to 400 F.

Line two large baking sheets with parchment paper and spray cooking spray. Place the wings in a large bowl drizzle with olive oil and mix to coat. Sprinkle the seasoning, corn starch, and salt over the chicken and mix until coated. Arrange the wings on the baking sheet in a single layer without touching. Bake for 45 minutes, or until internal temperature reaches 165 degrees and the skin is nice and crispy.

Easy Caprese

When you need an easy salad for an excellent appetizer a caprese salad is the answer. Fresh is best with this classic Italian salad made with juicy tomatoes, fresh mozzarella cheese, fresh basil, and a drizzle of balsamic glaze. Truly delicioso!

2-3 medium red tomatoes
12 oz fresh mozzarella cheese
1 T. balsamic glaze
⅓ c. chopped fresh basil

Slice tomatoes and fresh mozzarella into ¼ inch slices. Layer the tomatoes and mozzarella slices on a serving platter. Drizzle with balsamic glaze, then garnish with fresh basil and serve.

Cheesy Crab Dip

Warm, cheesy, full of Old Bay seasoning and lump crab meat. This crab dip will always be a crowd pleaser.

8 oz. cream cheese	1 tsp. lemon juice	1 T. chives (chopped)
¼ c. sour cream	2 tsp. old bay seasoning	½ tsp. hot sauce
2T. mayonnaise	¾ c. cheddar cheese	16 oz. lump crab meat (drained)

Preheat oven to 350 F. In a large bowl, stir together cream cheese, sour cream, mayonnaise, lemon juice, and old bay until creamy. Stir in cheddar cheese, chives, and hot sauce to taste. Using a spatula, gently fold in the crab meat leaving some lumps. Transfer the crab dip to a small baking dish. Bake for 20 minutes. Serve with crackers and enjoy!

Chicken Zucchini Minis

I am a total foodie, but I do try to eat healthy (most of the time). This recipe is for all my low carb foodies who want a meal or snack that is high in protein. And guess what? You get your veggies too.

2 c. zucchini, grated
1 lb. ground chicken
1 egg
2 green onions, finely chopped
1 glove garlic

¼ c. finely chopped parsley
½ tsp. dried thyme
½ tsp. season salt
¼ c parmesan cheese, grated

Preheat oven to 400 F. In a large bowl, mix zucchini, chicken, egg, onions, garlic, parsley, thyme, salt, and parmesan cheese together until combined. Place rounded tablespoons of chicken mixture on to a lined baking sheet spacing them about 1inch apart. Bake 18-20 minutes until the centers are firm. Remove from the oven and sprinkle with parmesan cheese. Set the oven to broiler then return chicken to the oven and broil until tops are light brown.

Soup and Some Veggies

Soup and Salads

Soup and salad are the perfect pairing for lunch, dinner, or any day of the week. It doesn't get any better than a warm filling bowl of soup full of veggies and protein. To jazz it up for you, I added some very cool salad combinations so you can have a sandwich or a quick side salad.

Split Pea Soup

Eat Your Veggies Broccoli Soup

Chicken in My Chili

Amped Up Chicken Salad

Strawberry Arugula Salad

Jazzed Up Egg Salad

Crunchy Cabbage Salad

Split
Pea Soup

25

Split Pea Soup

Whenever I have leftover ham, I always make this soup. This one pot meal is ready in an hour, and it is a favorite in my house. Full of vegetables and herbs we never get tired of it because this soup tastes better every day that you eat it.

Note: if you want to make this soup without the ham it will still be delicious. Just use vegetable broth instead of the chicken broth.

1 T. olive oil	1 tsp. dried thyme	salt, and pepper to taste
1 small onion, chopped	¼ tsp. dried rosemary	2 small carrots, chopped
2 celery stalks, chopped	8 c. chicken broth	2 c. chopped cooked ham (optional)
2 cloves, garlic, minced	16 oz. dried green split peas, rinsed	

In a large pot, heat olive oil over medium heat. Add onions and celery, and cook until tender for about 3 minutes. Add the garlic and cook for an additional 2 minutes. Add thyme, rosemary, chicken broth, and peas. Season with salt and pepper. Cover the pot with a lid and let the soup simmer for 60 minutes or until the peas are tender. Stir in the carrots and cooked ham, if using. Cook for an additional 20 minutes or until the soup thickens and the carrots are soft. Serve hot.

Eat Your Veggies Broccoli Soup

Ready to eat your veggies? Even if broccoli is not on your list of favorites, I promise you will be converted after tasting this soup. You will only need a few ingredients to create this creamy and delicious recipe that is sure to make you a broccoli lover.

2 T. butter	4 c. chicken stock	Cheddar cheese, shredded (optional
1 medium onion, chopped	4 c. broccoli florets	for topping)
1 rib of celery, chopped	2 carrots, chopped	
1 clove of garlic	Salt and pepper	

In a large pot, melt butter over medium heat. Sauté onions, garlic, and celery until the onions are soft, about 3 minutes. Add the chicken stock, bring to simmer. Add the broccoli and carrots stir to combine. Turn heat down to low, cover, and simmer for 15 minutes until the broccoli is soft. Transfer the soup into a blender or food processor and puree until creamy. Transfer pureed soup back to the large pot and continue to cook on low for 2-3 minutes. Add salt and pepper to taste. Serve hot with shredded cheese on top.

Veggies
Broccoli
Soup

Chicken In My Chili

Busy weeknight family meal, a potluck or game day, it doesn't get any better than a hearty bowl of chili. And why not try some chicken in your chili because this recipe is a great alternative to the tomato and beef-based version when you are craving something different. This chili is so good, you probably won't have any leftovers.

2 T. butter
2 T. flour
3 c. chicken stock or broth
½ c sour cream
1 c. half and half
4 c. rotisserie chicken, shredded or chopped
1 clove garlic, minced
1 medium onion
1 (15 oz.) can white beans, drained
1 tsp. dried oregano
1 tsp. ground cumin
½ tsp. chili powder
1 tsp. sea salt
1 tsp. pepper

Over medium heat, using a 4-quart Dutch oven or large pot, melt butter and whisk in flour. Add chicken stock and the remaining ingredients. Stir until well combined. Adjust seasoning to taste. Simmer over low heat for 15 minutes. Remove and serve.

Amped Up Chicken Salad

I love anything with fruit and nuts so I couldn't resist creating this chicken salad recipe that has a hint of sweetness, is full of chicken, cranberries, and walnuts. All those wonderful flavors and textures combined for a crazy delicious sandwich or salad.

2 c. rotisserie chicken, shredded or chopped
1 stalk celery, chopped
¼ tsp. garlic powder
¼ tsp. onion powder
½ T. dried chives
1 T. sugar
¾ c. mayonnaise
½ c. dried cranberries, chopped
⅓ c. walnuts, chopped
Salt to taste
¼ small iceberg lettuce, sliced thinly (optional)

Combine chicken, celery, garlic and onion powders, chives, sugar, mayonnaise, and salt in a medium bowl and mix well. Add cranberries and walnuts and mix to combine. Serve on your favorite roll or on a bed of lettuce.

Strawberry Arugula Salad

This salad is sweet, peppery, tangy, and crunchy. Perfect for a party or date night meal and the best part is you can mix it ahead of time and serve it up with your favorite meat.

Balsamic Vinaigrette
¼ c. extra virgin olive oil
¼ c. balsamic vinegar
1 T. honey
1 T. Dijon mustard
1 clove garlic, minced
Salt and pepper

Arugula Salad
10 oz. arugula salad (about 2 bags)
½ med. red onion (optional)
4 oz. feta cheese, crumbled
1 ½ c. walnuts
2 c. strawberries, sliced

In a large mixing bowl, whisk together olive oil and balsamic vinegar until emulsified. Whisk in the remaining vinaigrette ingredients.

Add arugula, red onion, feta cheese, walnuts, and strawberries, and toss to coat. Serve immediately.

Jazzed Up Egg Salad

Prepare to take your egg salad to a new level by adding my secret ingredient of ricotta cheese. Yup, just two tablespoons of ricotta cheese will change your egg salad from good to amazing. Give it try and thank me later.

6 hard-boiled eggs, peeled and chopped
2 T. ricotta cheese
⅓ c. mayonnaise
½ tsp. dried chives
½ tsp. season salt
Season to taste

Place eggs in a medium saucepan. Add enough water to cover all the eggs, then turn heat to high until the water comes to a boil. Immediately turn the heat off cover the pan and move from the stove. Set a timer for 12 minutes. After the timer goes off pour out the hot water and fill the pan with cold water to cover the eggs. Then add a large amount of ice cubes to the eggs and water. Let eggs sit in the ice bath until the ice has melted. Peel and chop the eggs. In a medium bowl, place eggs, ricotta cheese, mayonnaise, chives and season salt. Taste and adjust seasonings. Serve on toast or a bun with lettuce and tomatoes.

Crunchy Cabbage Salad

You are going to love this salad because it is the perfect side dish for dinner or for the cookout. Toasted ramen noodles and sesame seeds, crunchy cabbage and carrots are mixed in a home-made sweet dressing. Lots of flavor and crunchy goodness that comes together in minutes.

Cabbage Salad

½ head cabbage chopped
2-4 green onions
2 T. toasted sesame seeds (optional)
½ c. sliced almonds
1 pkg. of ramen noodles (uncooked) broken into small pieces (Save some to put on top)
Combine cabbage, green onions, nuts, and ramen noodles together.

Dressing

½ c. oil
3 T. vinegar
2 T. sugar
½ pkg. chicken flavoring from ramen noodles
½ tsp. each salt and pepper

Blend together oil, vinegar, sugar, chicken flavoring, salt, and pepper

Pour over cabbage salad just before serving.

I Sea You

Seafood

My son (AJ) and I have similar tastes in food. We love to experiment with a variety of flavors and cooking styles. So, when I am looking for something different to cook, seafood is my go-to item. This chapter consists of easy and flavorful seafood recipes that are some of AJ's favorites and are sure to become your favorites too. Add some sweetness to your meal with my Brown Sugar Salmon, and if there are any leftovers, use them to make some Soulful Salmon Cakes. Or get that low country vibe with some Cheesy Shrimp and Grits. If you love crab cakes, you have got to try my recipe for Jumbo Lump Crab Cakes, it will change your life. Are you hungry yet? Yup, I Sea You.

Brown Sugar Salmon

Easy Cheesy Shrimp and Grits

Cajun Fried Shrimp

Jumbo Lump Crab Cakes

Soulful Salmon Cakes

Brown Sugar Salmon

Add something special to your seafood menu by changing up your salmon with this recipe. This tender flaky salmon is drenched in a delicious brown sugar glaze and will be ready to serve in minutes.

2-pound whole salmon
3 T. melted butter
1 clove garlic, minced

1 T. brown sugar
1 tsp. Italian seasoning
1 tsp. ground paprika

1 tsp. garlic powder
1 tsp. salt

Heat oven to 375 F. Place foil on a large baking sheet, then grease with cooking spray. Place salmon skin down on the baking sheet. Combine melted butter and minced garlic. Brush half of the butter mixture over the salmon. Combine the remaining ingredients in a small bowl, and evenly sprinkle over the salmon. Drizzle salmon with the remaining butter. Bake salmon for 20 minutes, depending on preferred doneness. Remove salmon from oven, baste with juices, and rest for 5 minutes.

Cajun Fried Shrimp

If you love your seafood with a little kick to it, you are going to absolutely love this recipe for Cajun fried shrimp. This recipe is very easy to make and will be ready to eat in minutes.

½ c. all-purpose flour
1 ¼ tsp Cajun seasoning, divided
⅛ tsp. salt

¼ c. milk
¾ c. panko breadcrumbs

1 ½ pounds large shrimp, peeled and deveined
¼ c canola oil

Combine flour, 1 teaspoon Cajun seasoning, and salt in a small dish. Pour milk into a small dish, place panko bread-crumbs in a separate small dish. Dredge shrimp in flour mixture, dip in milk, then dredge shrimp in panko breadcrumbs, and shake off the excess breading. Heat oil in a large skillet or wok over a medium heat. Add half of the shrimp, and cook for 2 minutes on each side, or until done. Repeat with remaining shrimp. Serve with your favorite sauce and side dish.

Cajun
Fried
Shrimp

37

Cheesy Shrimp and Grits

Let me take you to the low country. It's no surprise that shrimp and grits are a favorite comfort food among so many people. What's not to love about creamy cheesy grits with shrimp cooked in a flavorful sauce? Enjoy this southern comfort dish any time of the day.

2 c. low-fat milk
2 c. water
1 tsp. sea salt
1 c. cornmeal grits
2 T. salted butter
1 c. shredded cheddar cheese
Shrimp and Sauce
3 slices bacon, chopped

1 lb. large shrimp (peeled and deveined)
1 c. onion
1 clove garlic, minced
3 T. cornstarch
1 ½ c. chicken broth
1 c. heavy cream
1 T. butter

½ Tsp. cayenne pepper (adjust to taste)
½ tsp. hot sauce
½ tsp. sea salt
½ tsp. black pepper
½ c. chopped green onions

Prepare the Grits

In a large pot over medium heat, add milk, water, and salt. Bring to a simmer. Whisk in the grits and continue whisking until they begin to thicken. Continue cooking the grits for 15 minutes, stirring occasionally, until thickened. Stir in the butter and cheese. Cover and set aside.

Shrimp and Sauce

In a large skillet, cook bacon until crisp. Transfer to a paper towel line plate. Return to the skillet and add the shrimp. Cook for 1 to 2 minutes on each side. Transfer the shrimp to a plate and keep warm. Add the onions to the skillet and cook until softened. Stir in the garlic and cook for 1 minute. Sprinkle the cornstarch over the onions and garlic. Add chicken broth then cook until the sauce thickens. Whisk in the cream, butter, cayenne pepper, hot sauce, salt and pepper. Continue cooking until the sauce is thicker. Return the shrimp to the pan and cook for 3 minutes (make sure not to overcook). Stir in bacon and green onions.

Plate about 1 cup of grits, top with shrimp, then pour gravy over the top. Serve immediately.

Jumbo Lump Crab Cakes

As a Maryland native I can tell you that we don't mess around when it comes to making crab cakes. There are a few absolutes... First, you absolutely must have very little filler. Second, you absolutely must have fresh lump crabmeat. Third, you absolutely must mix with Old Bay seasoning and the right amount of additional ingredients; that includes my secret ingredient of melted butter for an added touch of deliciousness.

¼ c. mayonnaise
1 tsp. Worchester sauce
1 tsp. Dijon mustard
2 T. melted butter
2 tsp. Old Bay seasoning
2 lbs. lump crab meat
½ c. panko breadcrumbs
1 egg, lightly beaten

Drain and remove any shell pieces from the crab meat. In a medium bowl, combine mayonnaise, Worchester sauce, mustard, melted butter, and Old Bay seasoning. Gently fold in crab meat, panko breadcrumbs, and egg. Mix lightly until moist, trying not to break apart any crab meat lumps.

Line a baking sheet with aluminum foil and lightly grease with cooking spray. Carefully form 8 jumbo cakes. Place the crab cakes on the baking sheet.

Preheat the broiler to high heat. Place crab cakes on top rack, broil for about 7-8 minutes. Remove crab cakes from the boiler and transfer to a serving plate. Garnish with a sprinkle of Old Bay seasoning. Serve with your favorite dipping sauce and enjoy!

Soulful Salmon Cakes

Trust me... it will be worth it to cook your salmon for this recipe because using freshly cooked or leftover salmon combined with my recipe is what will make your salmon cakes soulful. If you just don't have any fresh salmon, you can use the can version. I guarantee there won't be any leftovers.

1 ½ tsp. Dijon mustard
½ tsp. chicken bouillon powder
⅓ c celery, diced and sautéed
½ c. onion, diced and sautéed
1 tsp salt
1 lb. cooked salmon or two 6 oz. cans of skinless pink salmon
1 egg, beaten
½ c. crackers, crushed
6 T. cooking oil

In a medium bowl, thoroughly mix all ingredients together except cooking oil. Refrigerate for 15 minutes then shape into 10 patties. Heat a medium skillet over medium heat. Add 6 tablespoons of cooking oil to the pan. Fry patties until golden brown about 2 minutes on each side. Drain cooked patties on a paper towel-lined plate. Serve hot with some tartar sauce.

We are Beefing

Meats

We are beefing in a good way because I have some recipes in this chapter that will make you happy. The Beef Tenderloin is a bit pricy, but it is the perfect holiday or special occasion meat that will never disappoint. The Pot Roast and Beef Short Ribs are awesome one-pot meats that will save you time in the kitchen for a couple of days. And when you want to try something different with ground beef, my Hamburger Delight is economical, easy, and delicious.

Delectable Beef Tenderloin

Sop It Up Pot Roast

Hamburger Delight

Pan Seared Rib-Eye

Succulent Beef Short-Ribs

Beefy Noodles

Delectable
Beef
Tenderloin

43

Delectable Beef Tenderloin

This delectable beef tenderloin is always a staple on my holiday, special occasion, or celebration menu. Yes, beef tenderloin is expensive but after you are over the sticker shock, prepare yourself for a treat because it is worth every penny, and you will have enough to feed a crowd. The last piece of good news is that to make this easy, elegant, melt-in your-mouth beef you will only need three ingredients and don't forget your meat thermometer to ensure that it is cooked to perfection.

2 – 3 lbs. beef tenderloin, (fat and silver skin removed)
2 T. Kosher salt
1 ½ tsp. coarsely ground black pepper

2 T. olive oil
Let the tenderloin stand at room temperature for 1 hour before roasting.

Preheat oven to 450 F. Heat a large skillet over medium heat. Rub beef with olive oil, and cover all sides with salt and pepper. Place beef in skillet, and brown on all sides, about 3 minutes. Transfer beef to a large roasting pan. Roast uncovered for 25 minutes or until a thermometer inserted in the center reads 125 F. Remove from oven and let the beef rest for 15 minutes before slicing.

Sop It Up Pot Roast

When you want a hearty rib sticking meal this tender delicious roast will hit the spot. I promise you will be sopping up everything on your plate.

¾ c. all-purpose flour
2–3-pound boneless beef chuck roast
1 tsp. sea salt
1 tsp. black pepper

1 T. olive oil
1 large onion, diced and quartered
3 medium carrots, cut into large chunks

3 c. yellow potatoes, peeled and cubed
3 c. beef broth
Parsley for garnish

Preheat oven to 300 F. Combine flour, salt and pepper. Cover roast on all sides with the flour mixture. Heat oil over medium heat in a large pot or Dutch oven. Brown roast on all sides for about 10 minutes, then remove from pot and set aside. Add onions and carrots to the pot. Reduce the heat to medium and cook for about 4 minutes or until the onions are soft. Add the potatoes and place the roast on top of the vegetables. Add beef broth to the pot. Cover with a lid and transfer to the oven. Cook for 3 hours or until meat falls apart with a fork.

Remove roast from pot, garnish with parsley, and serve with vegetables, mashed potatoes, and sauce.

Sop It Up
Pot
Roast

Hamburger Delight

Let your hamburger help you. Full of flavor, this recipe is perfect for busy weeknights or for when you need a quick filling meal.

1 lb. ground beef
1 medium onion, chopped
2 tsp. dried thyme
¾ tsp. salt

¼ tsp. black pepper
½ c. water
14 oz. beef broth, divided
8 oz. penne pasta noodles

2 T. flour
½ c. sour cream
1 T. dried parsley for garnish

Cook ground beef over medium heat, breaking it up with a wooden spoon until no longer pink. Stir in chopped onion, thyme, salt, and pepper, for about 5 minutes until onions have softened. In a separate pot, bring water, 1 ½ cup beef broth, and penne pasta to a boil. Cook pasta stirring occasionally until tender, 8 to 10 minutes.

In a small bowl, whisk the flour with the remaining ¼ cup of broth until smooth, and stir into the hamburger mixture. Add in the cooked penne pasta and sour cream to the hamburger mixture then simmer stirring often until the sauce is thickened. Garnish with parsley.

Pan-Seared Rib-Eye Steak

No fancy ingredients needed to turn your kitchen into a steak house. You can't go wrong with a tender juicy ribeye steak basted in butter with a hint of garlic. Just pull out your cast iron skillet and get ready to impress.

2 (16 oz.) Ribeye steaks
2 tsp. season salt
1 tsp. black pepper
1 T. olive oil
2 T. salted butter, at room temperature
1 clove garlic, crushed

Let steak stand at room temperature for 30 minutes. Sprinkle with season salt and pepper evenly over steaks. Heat a cast iron skillet over high heat. Add oil to pan. Add steaks to the pan and cook for 3 minutes on each side or until brown. Reduce heat to medium, and add butter and garlic to the pan. Using an oven mitt, tilt the pan and baste the steaks with butter. Remove steaks from the pan, and pour the butter mixture over them. Cover loosely with foil and let stand for 10 minutes. Cut steaks diagonally against the grain into thin slices.

Succulent Beef Short-Ribs

Here is a dish that you would pay top dollar for in a restaurant, but I am going to help you create the same experience at home. You will only need one pot, and a few ingredients cooked low and slow for three hours. The result is fall off the bone deliciousness.

2-3 pounds beef short ribs	1 T. garlic powder	4 c. beef broth
Season salt and pepper to taste	1 T onion powder	2 carrots, chopped
	2 T. butter	1 small onion, chopped
	2 c. red wine	

Preheat oven to 325 F. Pat ribs dry, then sprinkle season salt, pepper, garlic powder, and onion powder on all sides. Melt 2 tablespoons butter in a large Dutch oven. Add ribs and brown on all sides. Remove ribs. Pour in red wine, and boil until it reduces to about 1 cup. Add ribs back into the pot along with the wine and beef broth and bring to a boil. Cover the pot and bake for 2.5 hours; then add carrots and onions. Continue cooking for 30 minutes or until the meat falls off the bone.

*Jazz up this dish and serve over rice or mashed potatoes.

Beefy Noodles

This recipe adds something extra special to your typical beef and noodles entree. Mushrooms, onions, tender beef, and a wine sauce are to die for over perfectly cooked noodles. Your weeknight meal just got better.

2 tsp. butter
½ lb. beef sirloin steak cut into ½ inch thick strips
2 T. diced onion
1 ½ c. mushrooms, cut into quarters

¾ c. red wine or beef broth
¼ c. plus 2 T. water, divided
3 T. chopped fresh parsley
¼ tsp. salt

⅛ tsp. pepper
2 c. uncooked pasta or egg noodles (about 4 oz.)
1 T. all-purpose flour

In a Dutch oven or a large skillet, heat butter over medium-high heat; sauté beef and onion until beef is lightly browned, 1-2 minutes. Stir in mushrooms, wine, ¼ cup water, 2 Tbsp. parsley and seasonings; bring to boil. Then reduce heat; simmer, covered, until beef is tender, about 1 hour.

While beef is cooking, prepare noodles according to package instructions. Drain

In a small bowl, mix flour and the remaining water until smooth; stir into beef mixture. Bring to a boil; cook and stir until thickened, about 2 minutes. Serve over your favorite pasta or noodles. Sprinkle with remaining parsley.

Chicken Man

Poultry

My husband loves chicken (especially fried chicken wings), so I had to get creative to broaden his chicken palate. This chapter is dedicated to my chicken man and to all the chicken lovers because you will find chicken meals for days prepared in all kinds of ways. My Crispy Oven Fried Chicken serves up that fried chicken experience without the grease, shh, don't say anything because my chicken man can't tell the difference. Ease in some vegetables with my Chicken Squash Bake or Chicken Lasagna. If you are short on time, try the Easy Chicken Enchiladas, or sweeten it up with some Sweet and Spicy Chicken. Chicken Man mission accomplished.

Sweet and Spicy Chicken

Crispy Oven Fried Chicken

Chicken Lasagna

Chicken Squash Bake

Easy Chicken Enchiladas

Chicken Fried Rice

Sweet and Spicy Chicken

Sweet and Spicy Chicken

You will get invited back to the cookout with this sweet and spicy chicken dish. Serve it up with a vegetable, some potato salad, and beans. This one is a winner.

2 tsp. season salt
2 tsp. garlic powder
1 tsp. chili powder
½ tsp. ground cumin

1 tsp. paprika
¼ tsp. ground red pepper
8-piece chicken thighs or chicken parts

Cooking spray
¼ c. honey
2 tsp. cider vinegar

Preheat broiler. Combine the first 6 seasoning ingredients in a large bowl. Add chicken to the bowl, and cover with seasonings. Place chicken on a broiler pan covered with foil, and coat with cooking spray. Broil chicken for 5 minutes on each side. Combine honey and vinegar in a small bowl, and stir well until mixed. Remove chicken from oven and brush with half of honey mixture. Broil for an additional minute, then remove and brush with the remaining honey mixture. Broil for one additional minute or until the chicken is done.

Crispy Oven Fried Chicken

There is nothing like the smell and taste of fried chicken and I have got a recipe that you are going to love. No greasy frying necessary because your chicken will get crispy in the oven. Dinner time just got more delicious.

2 pounds chicken
2 eggs, beaten
½ c. all-purpose flour
1 tsp. corn starch

2 tsp. brown sugar
1 tsp. smoked paprika
½ tsp. chili powder
½ tsp. garlic powder

½ tsp. onion powder
Season salt and pepper to taste
Cooking spray

Preheat oven to 425 F. Place chicken pieces in the egg mixture to coat. Add flour, corn starch, brown sugar and all the spices to a zip-lock bag; then add in the chicken. Shake until fully covered. Line a sheet pan with foil and spray with cooking spray or use a well-greased cast iron skillet. Add the chicken to the pan or skillet. Bake the chicken for 15-20 minutes, then flip chicken and spray with cooking spray. Bake for an additional 15 minutes or until the chicken is crisp and cooked throughout. Remove from the oven and allow chicken to rest for 5 minutes before serving.

Crispy
Oven Fried
Chicken

Chicken Lasagna

Calling all lasagna lovers, chicken lovers and cheese lovers this dish is for you.

5 c. shredded cooked rotisserie chicken
1 T. olive oil
1 medium onion
4 T. butter
⅓ c. all-purpose flour
2 ½ c. chicken broth

2 ½ c. milk or half and half
4 oz. fresh spinach, chopped
9 lasagna noodles, cooked
2 tsp. sea sal
½ tsp. black pepper
2 cloves garlic, minced
15 oz. ricotta cheese

1 egg
¼ c. parsley
¼ c. parmesan cheese
3 c. mozzarella cheese (reserve 1 cup
for topping)

Preheat oven to 375 F. Cook pasta according to package instructions in a large pot of salted water until al dente. Then drain hot water and add cold water to the pot to stop the cooking process and prevent noodles from sticking together. Shred 5 cups of chicken.

Spinach Sauce: Place a large saucepan over medium heat, add olive oil, and sauté onions for 3-4 minutes or until soft. Add butter and whisk in flour for 3 minutes. Add chicken broth, half/half, salt and pepper. Whisk until smooth and simmer for 5 minutes until thickened to a light gray consistency. Add minced garlic and chopped spinach and stir to combine then remove from heat.

Ricotta cheese sauce: In a large bowl, whisk together ricotta, egg, 2 cups mozzarella cheese, ¼ cup parmesan, and ¼ cup of parsley.

Assemble Chicken Lasagna and Bake

Spinach sauce

9 lasagna noodles, cooked

Ricotta cheese sauce

Shredded chicken

Add a little spinach sauce to cover the bottom of a 9x13-casserole dish, top with 3 noodles, add half of the ricotta sauce, and half of the shredded chicken, then ladle with a third of the spinach sauce, add a second layer of noodles, ricotta cheese, shredded chicken and spinach sauce. Add the remaining three noodles, and sauces. Sprinkle the top with a cup of reserved cheese. Cover and bake on center rack for 45 minutes, then uncover and boil for 3 minutes to brown cheese. Let lasagna rest for 10 minutes uncovered before serving.

Chicken Squash Bake

Use up all that zucchini and squash from your garden with this easy and delicious recipe. This dish comes together quickly so that it saves you time in the kitchen and it freezes well too.

3 T. butter
3 yellow squash, sliced ¼ inch thick
¼ c. chopped onion
2 c. cooked chicken
2 tsp. sea salt
2 eggs, lightly beaten
1 c. sour cream
1 c. shredded cheddar cheese
½ c. shredded Swiss cheese
½ c. mayonnaise
½ tsp. dried thyme
½ tsp. black pepper
¼ c. grated parmesan cheese
2 sleeves crackers, crushed

Preheat oven to 350 F. Lightly spray 12x7 inch baking dish with cooking spray. Set aside. In a large skillet, melt 3 T. butter over medium heat. Add squash, onion, and salt. Cook until squash is tender, for about 10 minutes. Drain squash mixture in a colander for 5 minutes, then add chicken. In a large bowl, mix eggs, and the next six ingredients (through to pepper). Add cooked squash and chicken mixture. Pour the mixture into the prepared baking dish. Melt the remaining 3 T. butter. Combine crushed crackers, melted butter, and Parmesan cheese, then sprinkle over the casserole. Bake uncovered for 20 minutes.

Easy Chicken Enchiladas

These easy chicken enchiladas will become your go-to recipe when you have a taste for some Mexican food.

Enchilada Filing

1 T. olive oil

2 c. chopped or shredded cooked chicken

15 oz. can black beans, rinsed

1 tsp. chili powder

½ tsp. ground cumin

½ tsp. onion powder

½ tsp. dried oregano

1 tsp. season salt

1 (28 oz. can) enchilada sauce (mild or hot)

12 oz. shredded cheese (about 3 cups)

6-8 large flour tortillas

Preheat oven to 350 F. In a large bowl, combine cooked chicken, black beans, chili powder, cumin, onion powder, dried oregano, season salt, and 1 cup of the enchilada sauce. Stir until well combined.

Assemble the Enchiladas

15 oz. can enchilada sauce

½ c. shredded cheese

Spread ½ c. of enchilada sauce over the bottom of a greased 13x9 inch baking dish. To assemble the enchiladas, put ⅓ cup of the chicken and bean mixture in the middle of the tortilla. Top with about desired amount of cheese. Roll up the tortilla tightly. Place the enchilada seam-side down in the prepared baking dish. Repeat with remaining tortillas, enchilada filling, and cheese. Spread the remaining sauce over the tops of the enchiladas, then sprinkle with cheese. Bake enchiladas for 20-25 minutes, until hot and bubbly. Let enchiladas rest for 5 minutes, then serve with your favorite toppings.

Note: Take a shortcut and use store-bought rotisserie chicken or any cooked chicken will work in this recipe.

Chicken Fried Rice

Leftover rotisserie chicken? No problem because you are going to love this easy fried rice recipe. Go ahead and get creative because another beautiful thing is that you can add in whatever meat, seafood, or vegetables that you have on hand.

Sauce
½ tsp. cornstarch
 2 T. soy sauce
1 T. honey
1 tsp. canola oil
1 garlic clove, minced

Fried Rice
canola oil
2 eggs
2 green onions, cut into pieces
2 c. hot cooked brown rice
2 c. rotisserie chicken, cut into cubes

For the sauce: mix first five ingredients together; then set aside.

Fried Rice: In a large skillet, heat canola oil over a medium-high heat; stir-fry eggs and break into small pieces then set aside. Add 1-2 tablespoon of oil and cook green onions until tender, about 1-2 minutes. Add in cooked rice, cooked eggs, and chicken. Stir sauce mixture and add to the skillet and mix until well heated. Serve and enjoy.

Slide over the Sides

Side Dishes

This chapter is dedicated to my mother, Esther, also affectionately called Puddie and Mama by her grandchildren. My Mom was a beautiful caring person and a wonderful cook. At an early age, I was her sous chef and she taught me the rules of the kitchen and cultivated my love for cooking. To this day, I still wear an apron when I cook, I always cook a Sunday dinner, I clean up as I go, and I always sweep the floor when I am done. Family gatherings always made Mom happy and good food, mainly the side dishes of corn pudding, mac and cheese, and sweet potatoes were a family favorite. Even though I know her recipes by heart, I still pull out Mom's handwritten notes when I am cooking. It feels like a warm hug from her. Thanks, Mom!

Puddies Corn Pudding

Homemade Fettuccine Alfredo

Bring On The Brussels Sprouts

Mac and Cheese Please

Loaded Mashed Potatoes

Pass the Potatoes

Sassy Sweet Potato Casserole

Puddies
Corn
Pudding

63

Puddies Corn Pudding

My mother always put a lot of love in her corn pudding. Sweet, creamy, comforting, and delicious. This can be the perfect side dish or even a dessert.

¼ c. butter, melted
1 (14.75 oz.) can cream-style corn
2 eggs, beaten
1 tsp. vanilla extract

2 T. corn starch
1 (12 oz.) can evaporated milk
½ c. sugar
½ c. packed brown sugar

¼ tsp. nutmeg
¼ tsp. cinnamon

Heat oven to 350 F. Grease a 10-inch baking dish with 2 tablespoons of melted butter. Combine cream-style corn, eggs, vanilla extract, cornstarch, evaporated milk, sugar, brown sugar, nutmeg, and cinnamon. Pour mixture into baking dish. Dot with the remaining butter on top. Bake at 350 F for 30 minutes or until the knife in the center comes out clean. Best served hot.

Homemade Fettuccini Alfredo

No major cooking skills needed for you to make this recipe, you only need a few ingredients and a few minutes. Serve it up as a side dish or top it with some chicken or seafood for an impressive meal.

1 (9-oz.) package of fettuccine pasta
1 clove garlic, minced
2 tsp. olive oil

½ c. grated Parmigiano cheese
⅓ c. half/half
3 T. cream cheese

¼ tsp. black pepper
1 T. chopped parsley

Cook fettuccine pasta according to package directions. Drain pasta in a colander, reserving ¼ c. of cooking liquid. In a large skillet over medium heat, add oil and garlic to the pan, stirring occasionally. Remove garlic from the pan. Reduce heat to medium. Add reserved cooking liquid, Parmigiano cheese, half/half, cream cheese, and pepper to pan, and cook for 2 minutes or until cheese melts. Combine pasta, and cheese mixture. Sprinkle with parsley.

Homemade Fettuccini Alfredo

Bring on the Brussels Sprouts!

This recipe is a delicious way to turn anyone into a brussels sprouts lover.

4 slices of bacon, finely chopped (optional)
1 ½ c. sliced onion
1 tsp. season salt

1 T. onion powder
½ tsp. garlic powder
¼ tsp. dried thyme
⅓ c. chicken broth

1 pound Brussels sprouts, trimmed and halved
Maple syrup

Heat a large skillet over medium heat. Add bacon to pan, and cook for 7 minutes or until crisp. Remove bacon from the pan, reserving 2 teaspoons of drippings in the pan. Add onion and seasonings to the pan, and sauté for 2 minutes, stirring frequently. Add broth and brussels sprouts and bring to a boil. Cover and simmer for 5 minutes or until crisp-tender. Drizzle with maple syrup, then sprinkle with bacon.

Mac and Cheese Please

It took me a long time to get my macaroni and cheese the way that I like it, but after a lot of trial and error I finally got it right. This dish is very creamy and very cheesy, so forget about counting calories because OMG, it is so good. Whenever there is a family gathering, I always get a request for "mac and cheese please" so you can trust that this recipe is family tested and approve. I hope you love it as much as we do.

32 oz chicken stock
3 ½ c elbow pasta
*16 oz block sharp cheddar cheese (shredded)
*16 oz block monetary jack (shredded)

16 oz block havarti cheese (shredded)
16 oz mozzarella cheese (shredded)
2 c milk
1 ½ c heavy cream
3 eggs

¾ c sour cream
1 tsp each, onion powder, garlic powder
½ tsp salt
1 stick of butter

*Note: Use block cheeses and hand shred all cheese to ensure a creamier mac and cheese.

Preheat oven to 375 degrees F. Lightly grease a 9x13 baking dish. Set aside.

Cook elbow macaroni in the chicken stock until al dente (about 6-7 minutes). While macaroni is cooking, use a grater to hand shred all the cheese into a bowl. Set aside.

Strain water from the cooked macaroni, then transfer into a large bowl. Add butter, 1 cup of cheese, sour cream, onion powder, garlic powder and salt. Gently stir to combine.

Custard: In a separate bowl, whisk together milk, heavy cream, and eggs.

Layer evenly in the baking dish, 2 cups of macaroni, 2 cups of cheese, and 1 cup of custard mixture.

Continue the layering process until the desired amount of ingredients are used. Evenly sprinkle the top of macaroni and cheese with the remaining cheese.

Bake uncovered at 375 degrees for 45 minutes. Cool for 15 minutes before serving.

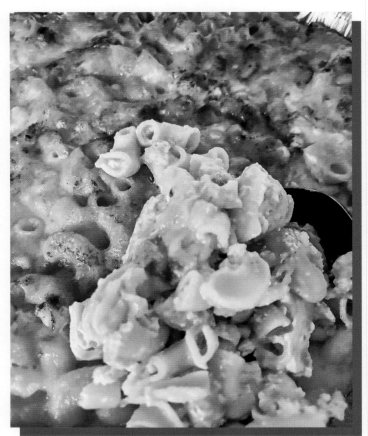

Loaded Mashed Potatoes

There is nothing like homemade mashed potatoes as the perfect side dish.

2 pounds Yukon gold potatoes, coarsely chopped
½ c. milk
½ c. (2 oz.) shredded sharp cheese
½ sour cream
2 slices bacon, cooked and finely chopped (optional)
½ tsp. black pepper
1 tsp. sea salt

Place potatoes in a saucepan, and cover with cold water. Bring to a boil. Reduce heat, and simmer for 15 minutes or until tender. Drain water and return the potatoes to the pan. Add milk, and mash with a potato masher to the preferred consistency. Cook for 2 minutes or until thoroughly heated, stirring constantly. Remove from heat. Add cheese to the mixture, and stir until smooth. Stir in sour cream and the remaining ingredients.

Pass the Potatoes

6 large red potatoes, cut into wedges
2 T. olive oil
1 T. garlic powder
1 T. sea salt
½ tsp. black pepper
2 tsp. parsley flakes

Preheat oven to 450 F. Place potatoes on a baking sheet, sprayed with cooking spray. Drizzle potatoes with olive oil, sprinkle with garlic powder, salt, and pepper, and toss well to combine. Bake at 450 F for 35 minutes or until potatoes are browned and tender. Remove from oven and sprinkle with parsley.

Sassy Sweet Potato Casserole

Sweet potato casserole always gives me a holiday feeling, but no need to wait for the holidays to enjoy this delicious side. After one taste, you will be making this dish all year.

3 medium sweet potatoes, mashed
½ c. half/half
¼ c. sugar
½ c. brown sugar

2 tsp. cinnamon
¼ tsp. ground cloves
¼ tsp. ground ginger
¼ tsp. ground nutmeg

2 tsp. vanilla extract
1 T. flour
½ c. butter, melted
2 eggs, beaten

Preheat oven to 350 F.

Boil sweet potatoes for 20 minutes or until fork tender. Remove from water and let them cool. Peel the skin off the potatoes and place the insides in a large bowl. Mash the potatoes with a potato masher and break up any large chunks. Add in the half/half, then mix until creamy. Mix in the brown sugar, white sugar, remaining spices, and butter. Add in the flour to thicken and mix well. Give the mixture a quick taste to make sure it is sweet enough. Using a mixer, add in the eggs and mix well, for about 2 minutes. Spoon mixture into a 9x9 inch pan. Set aside.

Sweet Potato Crumble Topping

½ c. all-purpose flour
1 c. brown sugar, packed
Dash of cinnamon
5 T. butter

In a medium bowl, add in all the crumble topping ingredients. Stir until crumbly. Spoon the topping evenly on top of the sweet potato mixture. Bake for 30 minutes. Then broil 5 minutes or until crumble topping is light brown and crispy.

A Bowl of Ice Cream

Desserts

I was always a "daddy's girl." My Daddy was a tall, slim, quiet, distinguished man who absolutely loved sweets. Every evening before going to bed, he would have a bowl of ice cream and some other sweets with it. The funny thing is, he never gained a pound. Now, I can honestly say that I got my height from my father, but I did not inherit the eat ice cream every day and not gain any weight gene from him. But you know what? I think he had the right idea because life is too short, so why not do what brings you joy? And my father's joy was eating ice cream and sweets every night. As I prepared the dessert recipes for this chapter, it felt like my daddy was smiling down on me as he enjoyed another big bowl of ice cream and that memory along with so many others warmed my heart.

Coconut Pound Cake

Scrumptious Strawberry Pie

Caramel Crumble Apple Pie

The Chocolate Lover's Cake

Same Day Key Lime Pie

Pass the Pecan Pie

Chocolate Banana Dips

Sugar's Cookies

Coconut Pound Cake

Coconut lovers, get ready for the mother of all cakes. I'm talking about a homemade cream cheese pound cake, buttercream icing and coconut on the top, middle and sides. I love this cake.

1 c. butter, softened
1 (8oz.) package of cream
cheese, softened

2 ½ c. sugar
6 eggs, room temperature
3 c. sifted flour

⅛ tsp. salt
2 tsp vanilla extract

In a large bowl, mix butter and cream cheese at medium speed with an electric mixer until creamy, gradually add 2 ½ cups sugar, beating well. Add eggs, 1 at a time, beating until combined. Stir in flour by hand until moistened. Stir in salt and vanilla extract. Evenly divide batter into 3, 8-inch or 2, 6 -inch greased and floured cake pans. Bake at 350 F for 30-40 minutes until the cake is golden or until a wooden toothpick inserted comes out clean. Cool in cake pans for 5 minutes, remove from pans and cool completely.

Buttercream Icing on the cake

1 c. butter, room temperature
4 c. confectioners powdered sugar
2 tsp vanilla extract
2 T. milk or heavy cream
2 c. sweetened flaked coconut for garnishing

In a large bowl, combine butter and powdered sugar; mix about 30 seconds. Add in vanilla extract and milk. Mix at medium speed for 1-2 minutes until creamy, scraping the sides of the bowl as needed. Add in additional milk 1 table-spoon at a time for a creamier consistency.

To assemble the cake: Spread a generous amount of frosting on the bottom cake layer and sprinkle with the desired amount of coconut. Continue the frosting and coconut process with the second and third cake layers. Then gently press coconut onto the frosted sides of the cake. Then slice a piece of cake and enjoy.

Scrumptious Strawberry Pie

I love a good strawberry pie and what I love even more is an easy delicious pie that I don't have to bake. My mouth is watering now as I think about the fresh strawberries, cream cheese and whipped cream mixed and folded into a sweet graham cracker crust. After you taste a slice, you will not be able to resist going back for seconds.

1 (9 inch) prepared graham cracker crust
6 oz cream cheese, soften
⅓ c. powdered sugar
¾ tsp. vanilla extract
2 c. frozen whipped topping, thawed
2 T. seedless strawberry fruit spread
½ tsp. fresh lemon juice
1-pound small strawberries, hulled and cut in half

In a medium bowl, place cream cheese, sugar, and vanilla, using a mixer beat at a medium speed until smooth. Fold in whipped cream topping. Carefully spread over the bottom of the crust. Place fruit spread in a bowl and microwave on high for 10 seconds or until soft. Add lemon juice and stir with a whisk until smooth. Add the strawberries, and toss to combine. Arrange strawberry mixture over the pie. Chill for 30 minutes before serving.

Caramel Crumble Apple Pie

My sister-law loves this recipe so whenever she visits us from Kansas, I like to surprise her with a pie. It's something about that caramel apple filling and the crumble topping dapped up with vanilla extract that makes it extra special.

Crust
14.1 oz. prepared pie crust (store-bought version)
Caramel Apple Filling
6 apples peeled and cored (Granny Smith or Honey Crisp)

½ c. sugar
⅛ c. flour
1 ½ tsp. apple pie spice
½ c. caramel sauce (store bought version)
Crumble Topping

1 c. flour
½ c. brown sugar
1 tsp. vanilla extract
1 ½ tsp apple pie spice or cinnamon
½ c. butter

Caramel Apple Filling

Heat oven to 350 F. Press the prepared pie crust into the bottom of a 9-inch pie pan and up the sides of the pan. In a mixing bowl, toss the apples with sugar, flour, and apple pie spice then pour into the prepared crust and spread evenly. Drizzle caramel sauce over the apple mixture. Cover with aluminum foil and bake for 45 minutes.

Crumble Topping

While the pie is baking, combine flour, brown sugar, vanilla, and apple pie spice. Cut in the butter and mix until it forms a crumb mixture. Remove the pie from the oven and sprinkle the crumb mixture over the pie. Place the pie back in the oven uncovered and continue baking for 15 minutes or until the topping is lightly browned. Allow the pie to cool for about 20 minutes, then drizzle with additional caramel topping before slicing.

Optional: Top with vanilla ice cream for pure apple pie pleasure.

The Chocolate Lover's Cake

Shout out to all chocoholics! Cake is served.

1 (18.25 oz) package of white cake mix with pudding
1 (3.9oz.) package instant chocolate pudding
½ c. sugar
½ c. vegetable oil
¾ c. water
4 eggs
1 (8oz.) sour cream
1 c. Semi-Sweet chocolate chips
16 oz. chocolate frosting (store-bought)

Preheat oven to 350 F. In a large bowl, whisk first 3 ingredients to remove lumps. Add oil, water, eggs, and sour cream stirring until smooth. Stir in chocolate chips. Pour the batter into a greased and floured Bundt pan. Bake at 350 F for 1 hour or until a toothpick inserted comes out clean. Cool in pan for 10 minutes, then remove from pan and cool completely.

Frost by spreading a generous amount of frosting over the entire cake. Sprinkle the top of the cake with a few chocolate chips.

Same Day Key Lime Pie

This pie is so good, it will be gone on the same day.

9 -inch prepared graham cracker crust
2 eggs
2 egg yolks
½ c. fresh lime juice or Key lime juice

1 (14 oz.) can sweeten condensed milk
⅓ c sour cream
1 tsp. grated lime rind
½ c. sugar
2 ½ T. water

In a medium bowl, beat eggs and egg yolks with a mixer on medium speed until well blended. Add lime juice and condensed milk, and sour cream beating until thick, and stir in lime rind. Spoon mixture into prepared crust. Bake at 350 F for 30 minutes or until firm in the center. Remove from oven and let cool on a wire rack, then cover and chill at least 2 hours before serving.

Pass the Pecan Pie

Brown sugar filling and chopped pecans in a pie. All I can say is Yum! Don't wait for the holidays to serve this pie because it is perfect to enjoy all year.

(14.1 oz) prepared pie dough
1 c. brown sugar, packed
1 c. corn syrup
⅔ c. old fashion oats

½ c. chopped pecans
2 T. butter, melted
1 tsp. cake batter extract (can also use vanilla)

¼ tsp. salt
2 eggs
2 egg whites, beaten

Heat oven to 350 F. Press pie dough into a 9-inch pie pan, draping the excess dough over the edges. Combine brown sugar and the remaining 8 ingredients (to egg whites) in a bowl and whisk well. Pour the mixture into the prepared crust. Bake at 350 F for 45 minutes or until the center is set. Cool completely before serving.

Banana Bops

Sometimes you just need a little treat to satisfy your sweet tooth. These bananas treats are easy to make and taste like a frozen candy bar that you just bop in your mouth.

2-3 medium bananas
1 c. (6oz.) chocolate chips (I like dark chocolate)
2 tsp. shortening
Toppings (can be anything you like): chopped toffee, coconut, sprinkles, chopped nuts

Cut bananas into six pieces (about 1 inch). Insert a toothpick into each banana and transfer onto a lined baking sheet. Freeze until firm about 1 hour.

Melt chocolate and shortening in a microwave; stir until smooth. Dip banana pieces in the chocolate mixture; allow the excess to drip off. Then, dip in the toppings; return to the baking sheet. Freeze for 30 minutes, then serve.

Sugar's Cookies

I love to experiment with all kinds of cookie recipes and share them with my family and friends. So, when family members ask me to make cookies, I always know exactly what cookie recipe they are referring to because there are a lot of chocolate chip cookie lovers in my life (especially my husband).

½ c. butter-flavored shortening
½ c. butter, softened
¾ c. sugar
1 c. packed brown sugar
2 eggs
2 tsp. vanilla extract
2 ½ c. all-purpose flour
1 tsp. baking soda
⅛ tsp. salt
½ c. miniature semisweet chocolate chips
1 c. milk chocolate chips
1 c. chunky chocolate chips
½ c. chopped pecans (optional)

In a large bowl, cream the shortening, butter, and sugars until light and fluffy. Add eggs, one at a time, beating well. Add in vanilla. Combine flour, baking soda and salt; gradually add to the creamed mixture and mix well. Stir in the remaining ingredients.

Use an ungreased cookie sheet and drop dough by tablespoons about 3 inches apart. Bake at 350 degrees. For 10-12 minutes or until lightly browned. Cool for 2-3 minutes then move to a wire rack to cool completely.

Menu Options

Weekend Brunch

Easy Cheesy Shrimp and Grits

Chicken and Waffles

Egg Stuff

Pumpkin Patch Muffins

Jazzed Up Smoothie

Date Night

Sweet and Spicy Chicken

Strawberry Arugula Salad

Pass the Potatoes

Same Day Key Lime Pie

Holiday Happiness

Delectable Beef Tenderloin

Mac and Cheese Please

Puddie's Corn Pudding

Bring On the Brussels Sprouts

Sassy Sweet Potato Casserole

Coconut Pound Cake

Hungry College Student

Egg Stuff

Crunchy Homemade Granola

Chicken Lasagna

Chicken in My Chili

Eat Your Veggies Broccoli Soup

Hamburger Delight

Sugar's Cookies

Game On

Lemon Pepper Wings

Teriyaki Meatballs

Soulful Salmon Cakes

Crunchy Cabbage Salad

Easy Caprese

Cheesy Crab Dip

Banana Bops

Chocolate Lovers Cake

Acknowledgments

Thank you, God, for guiding my footsteps and for all the blessings that you shower upon me every day.

My wonderful husband: Being your wife is the best part of my life. Thanks for always believing in me. I have accomplished so much because of your continuous love and support. You are my biggest food fan and are always excited about everything that I pursue. Thanks for also being the best barista, food tester, creative editor, and office assistant in the world. This book would not have been possible without your support.

AJ: My favorite son in the world. You planted the seed for this book, and you have truly been my inspiration. I have cherished every moment that we spent together on this project, sharing stories, tasting recipes, and making sure the photos were just right. Thank you for helping me with my computer skills and for your love and support.

Mom and Dad: Thank you for everything! Even though you are no longer on this earth, I feel your presence every day.

Michelle: My wonderful sister. There is never a dull moment when you are around. Thanks for the love, joy, and laughter that you bring to my life, and for always lifting me up with your spiritual guidance.

Stevie and D. Michael: Thanks for being the best brothers that I could ever have and for always supporting me.

Chef Gregory Cole: My partner in cooking. Thanks for inspiring me.

Aminah and Khalil, GiGi loves you.

Tania, Deidre, Fay, Carol, Linda (Dee), Traci, Kelli, and Brandi: Thanks for being my family food tasters. I am so grateful to have you in my life.

Shelia, Salina, LaRia, Karlease, Cynthia and Ladonna (LD), You are wonderful friends. Thanks for always believing in me.

Melanie Hauf: You are so talented. Thank you for sharing your creative genius with me on this project.

Crystal (Anointed Hands Hair Studio) and **Felisha** (Bomb Lashes), thanks for being a part of my glam squad and for your support.

Index of Recipes

About the Author

Stephanie Wilkins is a home chef, author, professional training director and creator of the Fulltime Foodie website. Developing flavorful recipes that help people experience all that food has to offer is her passion. Her recipes are easy to prepare, full of flavor and will fit into any type of busy lifestyle. Stephanie loves grocery shopping, singing very loudly while she is cooking and sharing a good meal with friends and family. She lives in Virginia with her husband and son.